HOW TO SELL
MORE
COOKIES,
CONDOS,
CADILLACS,
COMPUTERS...
And Everything Else

D0594731

HOW TO SELL
MORE
COOKIES,
CONDOS,
CADILLACS,
COMPUTERS...
And Everything Else

MARKITA ANDREWS

with Cheryl Merser

VINTAGE BOOKS
A Division of Random House
New York

Library of Congress Cataloging-in-Publication Data
Andrews, Markita.
   How to sell more cookies, condos, Cadillacs,
      computers—and everything else.
   "A Vintage original"—Tp verso.
   1. Selling.   I. Merser, Cheryl.   II. Title.
HF5438.25.A53   1986   658.8'5   85-40674
ISBN 0-394-74307-5 (pbk.)

Text design by Robert Bull

Especially for my Aunt Meredith McSherry
and also for
my mother and my Uncle Walter

CONTENTS

HOW TO SELL
MORE
COOKIES,
CONDOS,
CADILLACS,
COMPUTERS...
And Everything Else

INTRODUCTION

I was seven years old and in my second year of selling Girl Scout cookies when I learned my first real lesson about sales. The first year I sold cookies, I sold them only in my Aunt Meredith's apartment building because she knew everyone there. But by the second year I wanted to branch out, so my aunt and I went to another building in our apartment complex, across the courtyard from hers. There's a doorman there—he's still there—named Mike. I told him I wanted to go around with my aunt knocking on every door, because that was how I'd sold the year before. Mike said okay, but if he got any complaints he was coming up to get me; soliciting isn't allowed in New York apartments, and he wasn't exactly thrilled with the idea of setting me loose in his building. But he's a really nice man and I guess he figured: "She's just a Brownie, what's the harm in it?"

Sure enough, after we got up to the third floor, we buzzed this cranky old lady and she buzzed Mike: "So-and-so's soliciting." Mike came up to get us. I remember I was really upset; I'd only made it to the third floor, hardly any

Go where the customers are.

sales yet and I still had twenty-seven floors to go. But Mike told us to stay in the lobby to sell; we couldn't argue with the doorman, so we did.

It just happened to be the time when everyone was getting home from work—I sold forty-five boxes in way less than an hour. I couldn't believe it! It was the most I'd ever sold at any one time. When I was knocking on doors maybe one person in every six apartments would be home, and that isn't even a guarantee of a sale. Good exercise, maybe, but really tiring. I loved this new feeling of selling and selling and selling, then adding up all the orders at the end. I'm still grateful to Mike and even the cranky old lady. Ever since then I've been selling in the lobbies. And the first lesson about selling I learned now seems really simple to me: Go where the customers are!

My mother and I moved from California to New York City when I was six. I was just starting first grade and I didn't know anybody or have any friends yet. My Aunt Meredith, who lives with my Uncle Walter in the same apartment complex as my mother and I do, suggested I join the Girl Scouts, Brownies, actually. In that way I could meet people and get involved. Cookie-selling time in New York City comes in the winter every year, so the first year I was a Brownie I had the chance to sell.

My aunt had never seen a Girl Scout selling in our apartment complex—nine buildings on the West Side, over 4,000 apartments and lots of cookie eaters, we figured. We decided to start there. I didn't think too much that year about what I was doing or what selling was all about. And I didn't worry how many I would sell. All Barbara McLendon, my first troop leader, told us ahead of time was to have fun and just try our best to sell as many boxes as possible.

Which is what I did. I sold 648 boxes the first year.

By now I've done a lot of interviews on my selling techniques, and when I think about the methods I use to sell—and I think about them more and more—I can see that at the beginning it wasn't on purpose that I sold so many; at first it was by accident. Selling seemed like fun. At the same time I was meeting a lot of new people. My first year I don't remember anyone being nasty to me, which made selling seem even easier. People seemed to think: "She's a Brownie, she's so young, it's her first time, why not buy?" I sold to a couple of doormen who aren't here anymore, then I sold a box or two to everyone who was home when I knocked (no one complained about soliciting the first year), and anybody else I saw. My mother and my aunt bought the first boxes, to get me started. And I ate probably a million cookies myself, so after that I could really tell people how good they were.

I can see now that even in the beginning there were things I did right automatically— things I just knew somehow, things that the

other girls didn't. I was sort of surprised at first
that no one was selling as many cookies as I was.
Everyone in my troop was really curious and
interested. The other girls kept saying, "*WHAT!*
How did you sell that many? It's just your first
year here." And I kept thinking, "I just gave it
my best shot." Now, I think that I enjoy, I really
like selling more than most people do, which has
a lot to do with it. I certainly like selling more
than I like taking out the garbage—and I'm better at it. But I wasn't thinking about this my first
year in the Brownies.

Things happened fast for me after that. With
the help of Mike the doorman (and the lady on
the third floor), I sold 1,148 boxes my second
year, and Francis X. Clines wrote an article
about me for the *New York Times* (he bought
some cookies, too). When I was eight, my third
year of selling, I sold 1,754 boxes, and that's
when a lot more of the publicity began. I spoke
that year at a big corporate dinner at the Wal-
dorf-Astoria, a famous hotel in New York, given
to help the Greater New York Girl Scouts. It was
fun: I got to meet commentator Katie Kelly, Mrs.
Douglas MacArthur, and the actress Kitty Car-
lisle.

Mr. Martin Edelston, the publisher of a magazine for business people, *Boardroom Reports,*
was at the dinner, and he decided to write an
article about me. By now I wasn't a Brownie
anymore; I was a Junior. I still didn't understand
what an interview was. I thought I was just having a talk with a nice man, and Mr. Edelston is

still my friend (and customer!) today. He was the
first person to get me thinking about my selling
methods—nothing secretive, but he asked me
what I did. I told him and he thought mine was
a selling strategy that all salespeople can use. But
we'll get to that in a minute.

After the article appeared, I spoke at my first
convention, a meeting of the American Bankers
Insurance Group; I got to go to Florida for that
one. From there: more conventions (for IBM,
AT&T, Pacific Telephone, Million Dollar Round
Table, and others like that), more interviews—
more chances to sell cookies! And then when I
was nine, the Glyn Group (they had read the
article in *Boardroom Reports*) made a movie
with me for Walt Disney called *The Cookie Kid*,
which is still shown all over at sales conventions
for various kinds of companies. The next few
years my sales kept going up. And the incredible
thing was that selling was leading me in all kinds
of new directions. My whole family was wonder-
ing, "What does selling cookies have to do with
People magazine or a trip to Hawaii to give a
speech?" I thought it was amazing, too, but I was
having a great time.

I hope this doesn't sound like bragging. I
don't mean to brag or sound as if I know all there
is to know about selling. There's no way I could:
I'm only thirteen, and I haven't even sold yet for
a living (though I do babysit sometimes). But I
believe that selling is selling, no matter what you
sell. I've been at it for eight years, learned more
every year and have found, when I speak, that

people, even grownups who have been selling for years, are interested in what I have to say.

I haven't read too many of the other books on selling, but I recently went with my friend Cheryl (she helped me write this book) to a bookstore on Fifth Avenue, and we looked at the books in the Sales and Business section. There are tons of them! While we were there, I started to read a couple; they seemed to be written in some funny language, all full of technical terms and strategies to memorize. How anyone could remember all that I don't know. To me, selling is more about people than about following an exact plan where you don't even get to use your own ideas. My own strategy isn't something to follow word by word. It's made up of some things to keep in mind, or even in the back of your mind, when you're selling your own way.

And selling doesn't mean just selling cookies. You're selling yourself every day—in school, to your boss, to new people you meet. My mother's a waitress; she "sells" the daily special. Mayors and presidents trying to get votes are selling. My editor told me she had to "sell" the idea of a book on selling by a thirteen-year-old to her publishing company; a lot of people thought she was crazy! Then she had to "sell" the idea to my family—at first they thought she was crazy, too! One of my favorite teachers was Mrs. Chapin. She made geography interesting, and that's really selling. So maybe it's because I like it so much, but I see selling everywhere I look. Selling is part of the whole world.

In this book I want to talk about my selling method step by step: How it's worked for me and how I think it could work for other people selling cookies or practically anything else. There are other things I'm still figuring out, but for now I'll talk about things like: I-can't-take-it-anymore pressure . . . how not to be an "ostrich salesperson" . . . using your five senses when you sell . . . how the first thing you have to sell is yourself . . . how to think about competition . . . how to fit everything into your life . . . and how I would sell things other than cookies!

The magazine *TWA Ambassador* recently had an article about ten of the top salespeople, men and women, in the country—one sold shoes, a girl was selling peanuts to put herself through college, one sold pianos; I was in the article with my cookies. The article said that people who are "best sellers" are born with it, "like perfect pitch." I'm not sure that's true. I know that I love selling, but I also know that sometimes I get tired or discouraged and I just don't feel like selling cookies. I feel like throwing them. When that happens, when selling becomes work, you can't rely on perfect pitch or whatever it is. Then you have to use what you know, and remember what you've learned about selling. Everyone can get better at it; I'm still getting better—and that doesn't happen with perfect pitch. So here's what I've learned about selling. I hope it helps you.

CHAPTER 1

SETTING
YOUR
GOALS

Determination is what you feel when you have your mind set to do something. You're determined to reach this goal: You just have to. But you can't simply say, "I'm determined to sell nine hundred boxes of cookies today (or nine hundred spaceships)" and think you will. You might, you might not. (Probably not with spaceships.) A lot can get in the way.

For me it's better to think about everything that could go right or wrong ahead of time. Then I set my goals, short-term and long-term goals.

And then it's still not over because you have to keep changing your goals around depending on what happens: Was there a snowstorm today? Do I have a history paper due or extra homework? What you can do, what I do, is to sort out, really to separate, all the different kinds of goals —what you want to do today and this weekend, what you want to be doing in ten years. This makes it easier to keep track of what you're doing, whether it's selling cookies or anything else, day by day and also over the longer haul.

For example, one of my really long-term goals is to get a good job—a job that will make me happy (a selling job, of course, but I still don't know what I'll sell) when I get out of college. Even college is a long-term goal. Another long-term goal is to sell more than 40,000 boxes of cookies before I "retire." And every cookie-selling season calls for a new goal, too.

For a short-term goal: Say today's Saturday. I know I have the whole day free—and I know that if everything goes right I can take orders for at least two hundred boxes of cookies, plus still have time for lunch and some time in the evening to relax. I know because I've done it before. By the end of the day, my aunt and I will review the orders taken (we always add things up after selling). Then sometimes I'll think ahead, have daydreams about what I'll sell (and also get to buy!) when I get to the long-term goals. And knowing how I did, for better or worse, that particular day will help me to set the goal for the next selling day.

Then there are other goals, little side goals, that I always seem to have along the way—my Big Bird story, for instance. One year I found out that Mr. Carroll Spinney, the man who plays Big Bird, lived in my apartment complex. I had been trying and trying to meet him and sell him a box of cookies. It became a side goal. One day Fred, one of the really nice doormen, told me Mr. Spinney was home, and let me ring him up myself. His wife answered and I asked, "Could I please speak to Mr. Spinney?" He came to the intercom and I asked if I could come up to sell him a box of cookies because I would love to meet him. I told him I was a big fan and so are my cousins. He said sure. So I went up—he's on the top floor, which suits him since he plays a very tall bird; he seems happiest on a top floor.

Big Bird is wonderful! He drew me a little picture on the back of one of his Big Bird postcards, and he talked to me in Big Bird-ese with a little puppet. Later he even wrote to me at camp, and also to my cousin. Plus he bought a box of cookies from me, which is one of the best memories of selling I'll always have.

Other side goals might be selling to someone who has always said, "No, absolutely not, I will never buy cookies from you, no way, forget it!" or to sell extra boxes to someone who always makes you work way too hard and buys only one box. . . . But side goals are private; they're things you want just for yourself. You can't let them take over your mind. If I had just waited and waited to meet Big Bird that one year, I would have sold only that one box. I just build my side goals into my bigger goals, then forget about them till the right time comes.

I really have to concentrate most when I think about my short-term goals. They're the goals that add up, little by little. I can't just think, "Oh, I want to sell more cookies next year than I've ever sold." If that's all I thought about, I'd forget that I have to sell cookies this year first. It would be like thinking, "I'd like to graduate first in my class" but not working hard to improve your grades this term. Same thing if you're working for a company: You can't keep dreaming about how terrific it would be to be the president, because if you do you won't be doing the work it takes to get there. If you try to get away with "cheating" on your short-term goals, you'd better also rethink your long-term goals.

To say, "Oh, it'd be fun to sell seventy-five boxes of cookies today" is not the way to set a short-term, daily goal. You have to be realistic. There are more things to think about, whether you're selling cookies, doing homework, or I guess trying to accomplish just about anything else.

To begin with, you have to know how much time you have to work with. For example, when I sell cookies, I almost always wear my uniform. I think it's important, and it identifies me with the Girl Scouts. It's like a billboard. So when I get home from school and plan to sell, I have to change into my uniform; I may even have to iron it—maybe (I admit I do this sometimes) I've left it crumpled up from the day before. Just getting ready can take time.

If I'm selling in my lobby, I just take the elevator down, no problem. But if I'm selling at a company, my aunt will take me there in her car; we have to plan how long it will take to get there, even think about the time it takes to park, especially in New York. I also have to make sure I have everything I need with me. That means the order form, the card showing the pictures of the different kinds of cookies, proper change, etc. Mostly my aunt keeps all that stuff at her apartment, but we always make sure we have everything we'll need before we start. If I'm delivering cookies, I always make sure to have extra boxes with me so I can keep on selling as I deliver; every year I sell a lot that way.

We also have to remember that it takes time at the end of a selling day to keep track of the records. My aunt keeps the order blanks and the money for me; when it's all added up, she takes the money to the bank because we shouldn't keep it in an apartment. When I was little, my aunt would tell me how many I had sold each day; now I usually count it all up myself. My uncle told me it's important to do the records every day for two reasons: First, if you make a mistake it's easier to remember what happened and then catch it on the same day; and also, it makes you feel good to add up all the sales! So keeping our affairs in order is part of the overall plan, built into the daily goal.

I always set a daily goal because I know how

much homework I have, and if I set only one longer-term goal, say for the whole cookie season, I'd never be able to figure out how much I'd have to sell day by day. Some days, if I have a lot of reading to do or a test to study for, I can't sell at all. Then I have to plan the time to make up for a lost day, so I can still reach my goal for that season.

Even with a daily goal, though, things can go wrong. Some days, for instance, not that many people come through the lobbies where I sell or those who do just aren't in the mood to think about cookies. Maybe it's raining or snowing, or something horrible happened in the news, or there's a special show on TV that everyone wants to watch. I've seen all those things slow down sales, and it's really discouraging—but it's like dealing with rejection: There are some things you just can't do anything about . . . but we'll come back to that later.

Or maybe it's my fault that a selling day doesn't go well. Sometimes no matter how hard I try at least to *seem* cheerful, if I'm really in a bad mood, it just doesn't work. I'm not good at selling then; I'd be better off staying away from customers. Or maybe I've had a couple of bad selling days recently and I feel as if I have to rush to catch up. It's one thing when the customers rush me—that's okay. But I know by now that rushing a customer (even if there are several other customers waiting and you're afraid they'll go away if you don't get to them soon) usually means losing a customer.

When I was younger, I used to get carried away when I set my daily goals. I'd remember the best selling day I ever had and think, "That's my goal for today." I'd think that every single day. I don't do that anymore; it's not worth it. If all I think about is selling, selling, selling, there's no more fun in it. I look at the customers' faces and I don't see eyes, noses, and mouths; I see cookie boxes. Even when I'm grown up and selling for a living, I know I'll never forget this lesson. Setting impossible goals would be sure death or high blood pressure. You can sell as hard as possible but still have time for leisure and fun, for your friends, time to work off the stress of work. Selling should never be your entire life.

I've met a lot of really good salespeople at the conventions I've gone to, and I'm an honorary member myself of a few sales organizations, for example the National Association of Professional Saleswomen. The Million Dollar Round Table, which includes everyone who has sold over a million dollars (a million dollars!) worth of life insurance, has thousands of members; I spoke at their convention last year at Radio City Music Hall and got to meet a lot of people there. You'd think that all these people would talk about would be selling, selling, selling. But they don't. They talk about sailing, new restaurants, their families; they ask me about school. They have fun. Yet they're successful. I guess their lesson would be that when you set your goals, keep in mind that to be a success as a salesperson, you first have to be a success as a person.

A lot of people think I must be a really competitive person, or else how could I have sold so many cookies? What they don't know is that selling Girl Scout cookies is not a competitive "sport," and that the only person I'm competing with is myself. That's one reason the Girl Scouts don't keep track of sales on a national basis. Besides, I can't only think about cookie sales: My goals also include doing well in school, giving speeches, my other activities, this book—if I thought about selling cookies every minute of the day, I'd probably be a pretty odd character.

So when I set my cookie goals, both long- and short-term, I try not to think about how many this girl or that girl will sell, only how many I'll sell. Well, to be really honest, I have to admit that it *is* fun to sell the most, to be on top. And obviously, if you're selling for a living, you might have to sell a certain number, say forty-five lightbulbs, in an hour; or maybe you have to sell as much as the others in your position do. But I don't think a good salesperson would ever sell just to beat out somebody else. Besides, the best salespeople do a lot more than just sell the most —no matter what they're selling.

You know how these days there are more and more marathons and things like that? Sure, there were races in the old days, but they were relay races, games for fun, nothing so serious, not so much racing for money. It seems to me that it's more competitive today, thousands of people running, trying to prove something, prove to themselves that they're capable of doing something. It's scary. But what I like are the people who maybe don't finish in first place, but are really excited because they beat their own record or maybe just because they finished the race. They're running with their own secret goals. That's how I try to sell my cookies.

As for long-term goals, that's a little harder for me to talk about because I think long-term goals out in the "real world" are different from what they are for me at my age. I know that I'll be selling cookies for only a few more years, and I know that I want to sell 40,000 boxes altogether. I think I can do it. I'd like to keep giving speeches, too, because I meet great people that way and get to travel more than I'd get to do otherwise. I knew I wanted to write this book, even though it's a risk (more later about risks), because I thought it would be fun. I know I want to go to college, and then get a job in sales. I also want to buy a horse, but my uncle says I'll outgrow that one. Anyway, I have all those choices to make ahead of me.

If you're an adult, you have more real-world decisions to make. You have to decide if you want to get married, how much money you can or want to make, and so on. If it's a job selling, you have to know if you like to travel and how much traveling the job would require. If you hate New York City, maybe you should get a job in Massachusetts. Are you going to enjoy the job? Are you capable of doing it? Will it get boring after awhile? (For example, I think I might like to sell pizza or Walkmans for a summer, but not as a career.) Having all those decisions to think about makes it even more important to keep your goals separate, to know what you want for now and what you want for later.

My friend Mr. Victor Potamkin from Potamkin Cadillacs already offered me a job, selling Cadillacs. I absolutely love Cadillacs, so who knows . . . IBM—I've given speeches for them— offered me a job selling computers . . . American Bankers Insurance Group says I can sell insurance for them, and that could be in Florida . . . or maybe I might sell real estate for Andover Realty—I've given speeches for them, too—or sell books for Random House. Or maybe I'll end up selling something else entirely. You never know what you might be able to do in the future. But one thing I think is that it's better to be excited than worried about long-term goals; that's the whole point.

There's one more thing about goals. What happens if you've set your goal, figured out how much time you have—and all of a sudden you're selling more than you thought you would? That's happened to me. Extra referrals, invitations to sell at new companies, more speeches: But what about my homework? Sometimes there's just not time for everything. On the other hand, that's the most exciting thing for a salesperson; for a moment it seems that everywhere you look there are people wanting to buy from you. So what to do? Adjust your goals upward. Enjoy your success. And learn to use your time well.

It's
important
to keep your
goals separate,
to know what you
want for now and
what you want for later.

CHAPTER 2

USING
YOUR
TIME
WELL

I think it was the same year I learned about selling in the lobbies. I must have been seven or eight. My aunt and I kept thinking of new places for me to sell, and one day we were driving down 11th Avenue, on our way to pick up my mother from work; I had some extra cookies with me. So we drove into Potamkin Cadillac West (there's one on the East Side, too), and my aunt said, "Why not take this shopping bag and see if you can sell any in there?"

I remember I was really nervous when I first

walked in because it's so big. I went up to some people and said, "Excuse me, but would you like to buy some Girl Scout cookies?" They were amazed that a Girl Scout came to a Cadillac store. And they all said, "Sure, Girl Scouts. I'll buy ten boxes." I only had about ten boxes with me, so I dropped those and went running out to the car, *"Aunt Meredith, Aunt Meredith,* drive in, drive in, they're going to buy everything we have!" I was screaming my head off, and they were still saying, "A Girl Scout actually came here." I sold forty boxes (everything I had in the car) in about half an hour, and I've been going there to sell, and also to their East Side agency, ever since.

The season for selling Girl Scout cookies is only three weeks long, always in the winter, January or February. How it works, in New York anyway—it's different from state to state—is that we take orders all during that three-week period. The orders we get then count as our total amount for the season; the three people who sell the most in New York City get to go to camp for two weeks as their prize. Some of what we sell helps our troop, and some of the proceeds go to the Girl Scout Council of Greater New York, so that they can keep our camps in good shape and hold special events for Girl Scouts in the New York area. So it's all for a good cause.

After the three weeks, there's a catch-up time, where if there are a lot of people you've missed for some reason, or if there are more people you feel like selling to, you can just keep on selling. And you can order extra boxes to sell over the next few weeks. (My total sales include those I've made during the catch-up season, although I don't always count those that I sell to companies where I'm giving speeches.) Cookies sold during the catch-up period help your troop and the Girl Scouts, but don't count toward the camp total. In New York City, I've won the chance to go to camp every year.

There are several bakeries across the country that make cookies for the Girl Scouts. Some people think, "Girl Scout cookies, how cute"—but it's a pretty big business when you remember that there are over two million Brownies and Girl Scouts selling cookies every single year. Everybody has heard of Girl Scout cookies.

Last year we got the cookies in April, the quickest delivery I can remember. It was fun for me because the *New York Daily News* had my picture on the front page, and the cookies piled up to my aunt's ceiling.

Usually the cookies come in May and we're supposed to deliver them by June 1, for freshness and to provide good service. Still, three weeks is not such a long sales period—not like getting to sell all year long, whenever we feel like it—and we all have to work hard and sell pretty fast. Using time well was a lesson I absolutely had to learn to do a good job selling cookies. Otherwise three weeks would go by like *that*. There would be the same time pressure if you were selling Christmas trees, or bathing suits, or skis. My friend Annik, who works on publicity for Random House, says she has to do a press release for every book she works on before it's published. It's the same pressure I feel during exam time, or maybe the same pressure everyone feels in any job. A whole year can go by fast, so making good use of time is important for everyone, whatever you're doing. (Another example: There were a lot of things I planned to do while I was in the eighth grade; now I'm in the ninth grade and some of them still aren't done—time goes fast!)

Once I learned that selling in lobbies was using time well, I got pretty excited. I thought, where else do people go? Madison Square Garden, subways, all over the place. But I was only seven and couldn't exactly go all over the world by myself. And remember, first we take the orders, then we have to deliver the cookies afterwards, so it wouldn't make much sense to go to Brooklyn to deliver a box, then to the Bronx . . . talk about bad use of time! Better to sell in concentrated areas. So I decided to try the laundry rooms in my apartment complex.

Bad idea. People go to laundry rooms to do laundry. They're more concerned there with "whiter than white" than with cookies. And most of them go to the laundry rooms with exact change for the washers and dryers, so I'd have to follow any who did buy back upstairs for the cookie money, or go find them later. It got too confusing. And my thinking was pretty dumb, too, because the people who do the laundry are the same people who pass through the lobby.

They can stay in the laundry room for hours, and I couldn't sell cookies through all the wash, rinse, and dry cycles. So back I went to the lobbies, where I've pretty much stayed ever since.

After I had been around for a couple of years, people began to recognize me, at cookie time and also during the rest of the year. When they'd see me in the lobby in my uniform and with my cookie sign, they'd know: "Oh, you again. Must be that time of year." I felt like the first robin back from the Bahamas; must be spring. And I could see that knowing everybody is a really good thing for sales.

First of all, the more people you know the more fun your life is, and that has nothing to do with sales. A lot of people in New York, and probably everywhere else, too, don't even know their neighbors; but because of my cookies, I do. I live in a huge complex, but I say "Hi" to practically everybody, and I know all the doormen and the porters. And now I know people at my school, people at companies where I sell or give speeches, and other people I meet along the way. For a salesperson, that's an especially good thing.

It saves time when I'm selling to people who have bought before. Many times they'll just say, "Oh, I liked the peanut-butter cookies last year. I'll take two boxes of those." That's the quickest kind of sale—good use of time. I don't have to run through all the kinds, explain about delivery, etc. Of course, if there's a new kind that year I'll suggest maybe they'd like to try that kind, too, or try to sell them more in other ways. But the people who buy from me year after year are my real customers. I know that they like the cookies, that they like helping the Girl Scouts, and that they know I do my job. I'm not even selling, exactly, to these customers; I've already sold them years before. We're ongoing friends by now. And that's great use of time.

But even when you're starting from square one with a new customer who doesn't know a chocolate chip from a real live Brownie, you have to think about how to use your time. Explaining everything I know about Girl Scout cookies a thousand times a day can take forever (and get pretty boring). Is it worth it to sell just one box?

Yes and no. Yes, because one box is one box: It's a sale, and a sale is a sale. No, because to sell that one box you might have given up the chance to sell dozens of boxes to someone else who was passing by.

You know what it's like to be a buyer? (Even salespeople have to deal with salespeople.) Sometimes you know what you want; sometimes you don't. Sometimes you think, "I don't know what I feel like doing; maybe I'll just buy something." Sometimes you think, "I'm not going to buy a thing today," and then you end up with a new dress or boat and say, "How did this happen?" When the buyer ends up with something she didn't expect to have, a lot of times that's the work of a salesperson. A salesperson's job is selling, and selling takes time. So you would think that any time you're selling, or trying to, you would be using your time well.

Not necessarily. Enough can be enough. The salesperson always has to respect the customer, but the customer should also respect the salesperson. Selling is between two people, and it should work both ways.

One time, for example, I was selling in an office. They gave me only so much time to sell, and I was doing fine. You know how you get into a rhythm? Then I came to the office of this one man (I wish he had been in a meeting) and he said, "Okay, I'm going to buy a box of cookies from you. But first you have to give me your whole sales pitch." I said I would, but I knew: trouble. So I went through everything I could think of about cookies ("The shortbreads only have twenty-four calories, good for a diet . . ."). I remembered everything.

At the end, I was really tired—I had worked hard, believe me—but I felt good. He'll buy a lot, I felt confident. But no. He had one of those chairs that leans back and he leaned back. "I'll take one box."

"But don't you want some for friends, relatives; some to freeze for later . . . ?"

"I'll take one box."

Well, okay, that was what he said in the beginning, even without my sales pitch. But I couldn't help wishing he would have been more considerate. He knew I wanted to sell to the whole office, and there he was taking up all my time, even if he did buy one box. I thought about it later, when my aunt and I were adding up the sales. I was glad at least that I felt good about the way I pitched cookies to him; that was satisfying. Could I help it that I was selling to a brick wall?

Selling has its frustration points, like, I guess, all businesses do. In a way, it's the nature of the game: Every sale keeps you from another sale. And in sales you always want to know, what's going to happen next? Curiosity, I think, is a big part of selling.

There probably wasn't much else I could have done, stuck in that man's office, but often there's a better way for a salesperson to make good use of time with a difficult customer. Say you're selling shoes. A lady has come in and tried on thirty pairs; they're all piled up around her and you have no idea whether she's going to buy even one pair. The other customers are piled around her piles of shoes. You might say: "I'm going to leave you here with these thirty pairs of shoes for a few minutes, so you can think about what you need. Right now I have to wait on a few other customers who have been waiting. But don't worry, I'll be back." That's fair—to her and to you. But do come back. Who knows? She may buy all thirty pairs of shoes!

Or maybe not, but that's the way it goes. Sometimes, like it or not, just doing a good job can turn out to be bad use of time.

So sometimes the customer can make you waste your time. But you can waste your own time, too—by being too persistent, for one thing.

Being polite
and having good
manners are the most
important keys to selling.

But how do you decide when you're being too persistent?

If someone says, "Okay, I'll take two boxes," I usually say, "How about more?" and give them all the reasons to buy more I can think of—that's what selling is. But you can push too hard. I used to do that sometimes, to the point where they'd say, "That's enough, that's enough." That's not good. Now I watch the customers for cues about when enough is enough. That's making good use of time. I want to spend my time seeing other people, not just this one person who will buy maybe two boxes (and then maybe get madder and madder at me and never buy again).

Being polite and having good manners are the most important keys to selling. You can be persistent and polite at the same time, but learning that, at least for me, took some work. But then I realized that when I was pushing too hard I was doing it for *me*, for *my* sales. Bad use of time, bad treatment of customers, bad manners, too. You have to let people know you're talking to them and not just unloading something on them, that you're interested in what they have to say. You can hit all the bases—I always ask people who haven't bought in previous years if they'd like to buy this year (you never know), but I ask fast and only once. Otherwise it's a waste of time and it's bad manners. Oh, and I never, never push with older people. I just wouldn't.

Two of my grades went down (though two went up) this semester: bad use of time. I was selling cookies, giving speeches, doing interviews, thinking about this book, plus all the other stuff. But what did I leave for last? My homework. The most important thing. Too bad you can never see mistakes *before* they happen.

Using time well means putting every possible thing into perspective. You even have to know when to stop, when it's time for a break; maybe you just need to watch television for awhile. Also, just because you want to sell cookies doesn't mean you can ring people's doorbells when they're having dinner, or before they've had their breakfast, or when they're sleeping. And you can't just keep selling cookies when you're supposed to be doing your homework. You can't get carried away.

They say that time is money. (I say time is cookies.) Time is also people. Good use of time is not the same for people as it is for machines. A machine can go all the time; you can use it till it breaks. Sure, you have to take care of it, but you don't have to be kind to it. You're never using time well if people—your family, a friend who's depressed—don't come first. So the best use of time, in selling, life, etc., is taking care how you come across to the world.

CHAPTER 3

MEETING THE WORLD

I'm not in many classes with the most popular girl in my grade at school. I'm not in her clique either. But I understand why she's the most popular, with girls and also with boys. Everyone wants to be her friend. She's smart, gets really good grades. She's pretty and fun. And, mainly, she's nice to everyone, whether they're in her clique or not. (Our class is extremely clique-y.) When I see her she's so nice: She'll always say "Hi" and talk to me if there's time. She's that way with everyone. She's not a snob and she doesn't look down on people who aren't in her clique.

There are a few girls in my school who aren't nearly so nice. Girls who won't talk to other people unless they're in the "right" clique or who are always talking about others behind their backs. ("Ooh, look what she's wearing. I can't believe she's wearing pink socks and purple shoes with a green shirt," or whatever.) When the kids in my class were younger, before I came to this school, they invented cootie shots to protect against some of the really mean kids. Too bad cootie shots can't work as well when you're older. . . .

I've been going to the Chapin School in New York since I started fifth grade. I was so scared my first day—practically that whole first year. I was scared because I didn't know anyone there and I didn't know how they would treat me, whether they would be snobs or kind and thoughtful and try to help me out. For the first couple of days the school assigns girls to take you around to classes. That really helped. But even after those couple of days, I was still pretty nervous about going around alone. There were forty-nine strangers in my class. At first, some people made a point of being friends with the new people, but others didn't bother because they "didn't know anything about them." As for me, I thought if I didn't make friends in the first week, it'd be too late ever to make any friends!

But what does being popular in the eighth

grade have to do with selling? More than you'd
think.

The most popular girl in my class would
make a wonderful salesperson. She likes people,
and they like and trust her back. Her customers
would listen to what she had to say, and they'd
know for sure that she believed in her product.
She would never sell anything she knew was a
gyp; you can tell that about her right away. The
nastier girls, on the other hand, can't even sell
themselves. They put other people down to
build themselves up. Maybe they're insecure.
Whatever it is, you would know the minute they
tried to sell you something: This person doesn't
care about *me* at all; she's selling for other reasons. And you wouldn't feel good about yourself
if you bought so much as a bottle of shampoo
from one of them.

This doesn't mean that you have to be the
most popular kid in your class in order to be a
good salesperson—or to be a success. If it did,
only one person from every class could succeed.
What it means is that if you're not the most popular kid in your class, and most of us are not, you
will have to think about how you come across to
the world—before you even begin to sell,
whether it's selling yourself at a party or selling
hats in a hat store.

I know by now it must seem like there's way
too much to do—setting goals, planning time,
preparing to meet the world—before you even
begin to work at actually selling. But don't

worry; you won't have to get up at three in the morning every day to get all this going. Most of these things will become built into you after you've thought about and practiced them, over time. The thing is, say you're selling shoes. You want the customer to be happy with the shoes and also with you. You'll be connected with the shoes forever: You want the shoes to be good so you'll be proud and the customer will be happy. You also know that people keep on needing shoes, so you hope the customer will come back to you for shoes again. And after all, the customer meets you before trying on shoes, so *you* are the first step in selling.

You would think that the first thing people notice about you is how you look, how pretty or handsome or thin you are. It's true that looks are important, but I don't think that's what people notice first. Some businessmen are bald, for example, and many women in business I've met aren't all that pretty in the way we usually think of "pretty," like models or movie stars. What people notice more than looks you can't do much about are the positive things you do with the looks you have—and how confident, sincere, and cheerful you are.

If you're confident in what you're selling and you're sure that you want to do it and also sure that you're capable of selling whatever it is—go for it. "Sure that you want to do it" is the key phrase. If you know that you want to sell something, you can gain confidence by learning absolutely everything you can about the product.

You won't remember how shy you might be deep inside if you're having a good time with the customer, teaching him something, answering all the questions, and heading full blast toward the sale. A good thing to remember is that you can often hide your fears behind what you know.

In school, for example, one of my problems is that I don't speak out in class. Many times the teacher will ask a question and I know the answer. I sit there thinking, "I know this answer all right. I should definitely raise my hand *right now.*" But by the time I go through this conversation with myself it's too late. I can't get my confidence up in time. Someone else has answered the question. I'm letting my nervousness take charge, not what I know about the subject at hand. If I could instead concentrate on thinking, "I know this answer," then I could give the answer before I remembered I was nervous!

I know I'm more confident than that when I'm selling cookies. I'd never hold back and let someone else get the sale first. But when I'm selling, I'm not just me: I'm representing the Girl Scouts. I'm wearing my uniform, and I'm selling cookies for a great cause. It's still *me* selling the cookies, but I'm sort of the halfway point between the Girl Scouts and the customers, and it's easier for me to be confident selling than reciting in school. I tell myself if I can be confident selling cookies, then I should be able to speak out in school. But maybe different kinds of confidence come at different times.

There are ways to practice your approach to

selling that will help you to be more confident.
(Now, as I'm thinking about these methods, I can
see that I should try them out for school, too.)
For one thing, listen to your voice.

The first time I saw a tape of myself on TV,
I was so embarrassed! Here I was, this little kid
with a squeaky little voice. I sounded like a
mouse. (Who would buy cookies from a mouse?)
And I had this funny habit of closing my mouth
so that I'd hide my upper lip—that was nervousness, too. I could also hear that sometimes I
talked too fast: "Yeswehaveshortbreads." A lot of
people do that. Once I'd seen myself, at least I
knew what to work on. The mouse voice, I'm
happy to say, went away by about the fourth
grade. The rest still needs work, but I can tell
I've gotten better at presenting myself by looking at more recent tapes of my appearances on
TV and hearing tapes of my speeches (though I
still feel strange watching myself on video—
maybe we all do).

You have to sell yourself to sell your product.
Your speech should be distinct; what's the good
of knowing everything about your product if no
one can understand you? Or how will you come
across if you're always saying, "Um, let's see, uh,
um, yeah, we have, um, the shortbreads"? And
you won't know if you sound like a mouse unless
you listen to yourself. Almost everybody knows
someone with a tape recorder; you can practice
secretly to make your voice sound right to you.
And watch yourself in front of a mirror as you
give your pitch. I do that when I'm practicing

You have to sell yourself to sell your product, so dress to stand out (but not too much), speak clearly and naturally, make eye contact, stand as if you mean business—and remember your manners.

my speeches; or else I practice in front of my mother or my aunt. Am I smiling? Do I know what I'm talking about? Do I sound like myself or do I sound like I'm pretending to be somebody else? Even if my speech is memorized, does it "feel" like me?

Eye contact is another thing you have to remember. And *that* you can't really practice in a mirror, you just have to learn it. (Sometimes you can get away with looking at the customer's nose, but eye contact is better and more fun.) If you're talking above the customer's head, he won't be interested in your "lecture." But if you talk directly to your customer, showing just how much you believe in your product, he'll believe in it, too. One time an interviewer asked me if people bought cookies from me because I have big brown eyes. I was only seven and, in my mouse voice, I said, "Maybe they do and maybe they don't." Maybe the fact that my eyes are big and brown didn't have so much to do with it; maybe—probably—the fact that I use them directly to look into a lot of other brown, blue, green, and purple ones does.

People have noticed other things about my selling methods that I'd never even thought about. For example, I was selling in an office once this past year and a man asked me, "Do you stand that way on purpose?" What way? He said that the way I was standing made it look as if I wouldn't leave until he bought some cookies. (He bought ten boxes.) I didn't know I stood in a particular way; I don't think about how I stand.

(But after he said that, I couldn't stop thinking about my feet!) I realized there might be something to it: I know I prefer to stand, not sit, when I'm selling. You've been standing all your life, I know, but when you're selling, stand as if you mean business! It's all part of how you present yourself to the world, selling or not.

Another thing that comes up right away— more important even than confidence—is manners, common courtesy, being polite even if the customer acts like a barbarian. Having good manners is a choice you make; either you want to be polite or you don't. Also, you can't fake good manners whenever you feel like you should have them; the customer (or your friends) can always tell when manners are phony. But manners come up at every stage of selling . . . so more on that as we go along.

Confidence comes from inside, and manners, if you really mean them, will also come from there in the first place. Those things have to be worked on privately. What's fun—and easier—is working on how you look from the outside.

My mother bought a book recently about the royal family. When you look through it, you can always spot the queen right away; she's the first one you see in every picture. (Sometimes you notice Lady Di first, but she isn't in all the pictures.) The queen wears almost fluorescent-colored coats—bright blue, for example—when everyone else is wearing black or beige raincoats. You can tell right away: *Queen*.

My uniform does the same thing—well, in a

way. You don't see everyone walking on the
streets in a Girl Scout uniform, so it attracts attention to me and my product. What you want
to do is stand out, which will make your product
stand out, too. Singers and movie stars know this.
Or if you go into a bookstore and most of the
book jackets you see are brown or black, you'll
go right for the red book jacket. That's the one
that stands out.

But you have to be careful; you don't want to
stand out too much. Recently I was being inter-
viewed for *Le Figaro* magazine. The reporter
and photographer had come all the way from
France to see me, and we had a great time, went
all over New York City taking pictures and selling cookies. We were down on Wall Street one
day, selling cookies. Business was pretty slow. All
of a sudden a group of punks, about five of them,
came up to us. They were all wearing crazy
glasses; the men wore short ponytails; each one
had a different color hair! One of them said,
"Hey, wow, you're the Girl Scout who was on
David Letterman!" Then they all wanted their
pictures taken with me—five punks and a Girl
Scout. They were nice, but I doubt that I would
have bought anything they were selling, except
maybe some of the sunglasses. . . .

We wear uniforms at school, but even with
the uniforms some of the girls manage to look
special. There's Pink-and-Purple Day every year,
when we get to wear anything pink or purple
with our uniform skirts—you should see how totally different people can look even when they're

all wearing the same skirts. And even on regular days, some girls—still in the same uniform—really stand out, just by doing something out of the ordinary, an unusual hair clip, maybe, or a special shirt or pair of socks. Even from the head down you could tell us all apart: How we stand and walk, what we wear with our uniforms, whether the skirts are pressed or sloppy, and so on. To an extent, you can tell something about people by the way they dress—even in uniform.

I've heard the phrase "dress for success." As for selling, that would mean to dress in a way that makes you, and your product, look good. Not all blue suits and black ties; that's boring. And you have to dress in a way that will make you feel like yourself, so you don't feel like you're faking something. To sell well, you have to feel all ready to go out and meet the world!

Selling well is showing pride in yourself, your product, your profession. A tiny little store just opened up near my house; in it they sell a bunch of the things that everyone needs—shoe polish, umbrellas, envelopes. You'd have to know about the store to think, "Maybe they have what I need." But you *would* know about the store: When they first opened it, they put up streamers and banners and a sign that said *GRAND OPENING.* You couldn't miss it. The sign and all the streamers looked a little strange—the store is really small—and it reminded me of a birthday party. But the owners were introducing their store to the neighborhood. Like all good sales-people, they were *proud.*

CHAPTER 4

DRUMMING UP BUSINESS

One of my earliest TV memories is of Mr. Whipple, who (as you probably know) works in a supermarket but mostly hangs around the racks where they sell the Charmin toilet paper. I always liked Mr. Whipple: In the beginning he loved Charmin so much that he didn't want anybody else to have it, or worse, to squeeze it. I used to think it was so funny that a man who's supposed to be selling things wanted to keep everything for himself. Now, in the newer commercials, he's pushing the Charmin into ladies'

carts and making it look as though their babies
pulled it from the shelf; once he's got their attention, he tells them why they should buy it
(squeezably soft, thick, etc.). It's so different
from the early ads—still Mr. Whipple, but he's
finally learned to sell the Charmin instead of
keeping it all for himself. Talk about a lesson in
business!

Somebody told me that when traveling salespeople used to arrive in a town with their wares
for sale, they would bang on a drum to let the
people in the town know they were there. Then
the customers would come running. The salespeople were "drumming up business." Just like
Mr. Whipple sneaking the Charmin into the
shopping carts, or me finding new ways to sell
cookies, or like anybody who works in a store
who says, "May I help you?"

My best teachers drum up interest in their
subjects by telling us things like, "Math may not
seem like the most fascinating subject in the
world to you, but you'll need it in later life to
figure out your checkbooks, and also most jobs
require some math," or whatever. They set their
subject in the real world and we all think, "Yeah,
I'd better learn some of that."

There are a million ways to think about sales.
If you have a store, you have to get people to
come inside before you can sell them a thing.
You have to think about how the store looks inside and out, plus how you advertise, what you
say about your store in the phone book, what the
people who work in the store will be like—not

even to mention what you sell in the store and whether other people are selling the same thing, too.

Selling one to one is another thing. Sometimes I can just look at a customer and I know: mints; two or three boxes. Other times I start talking to a customer about one thing and end up selling the cookies with a totally different pitch. For example, maybe I'll be telling them that they can freeze the cookies for later and they'll tell me they're having a party. I stop telling them to freeze the cookies. Instead, I sell them dessert!

It's different if you're selling to a large group, or if you're selling over radio or TV, or if you're selling in newspapers: Half your customers might not even be paying attention to your ads. You have to draw in as many people as you can by making the ads appealing—then your customers will discover you. Or if you're selling over the telephone, you'll be able to talk and hear, but you won't be able to tell a thing from the customer's face. You sell with your voice and by listening harder than usual for the customers' doubts.

In my case sometimes I sell cookies to the people at conventions from the stage. I sold 5,000 boxes to the Million Dollar Round Table this way that time I gave a speech to their members at Radio City Music Hall. When I'm selling cookies that way, I can't see each person, just a sea of faces, so I have to tell them everything I know. I have to hit each question that *every single per-*

son might ask if he or she were right next to me.

But first you have to get to the customers, or get them to come to you. Better yet, meet them halfway. The drummer came to town, but the customers came to the drummer. When I sell my cookies, I go where the customers are, but once I'm there, the customers come up to me. You have to go where they are and then attract them —not kidnap them. If I were selling horses, I wouldn't set up shop on Fifth Avenue or in the lobbies of my apartment complex. I'd go to camps, farms, stables. (I like the idea of Markita's Horse Farm. I'd make a deal with carrot farmers to give a discount to my horse customers. . . .) Being in the right place at the right time is not usually a matter of chance.

As I've said, this was the first lesson I learned —finding my customers and setting up my cookie station in the lobby. But then what? A Brownie standing in a lobby just looks like any Brownie standing in a lobby—until further notice.

It's up to you to let the people know you're selling something. You can't keep it a secret. You have to attract the customers' attention, to you and your product.

There's a pizza place near where I live, where they do a great job of selling. You can't miss it. The sign is huge—red, white, and green, the colors of the Italian flag—and says *PIZZA* in big bold letters. There's a picture of a pizza with a slice missing, and you walk by and *you want that slice.* You can also smell the pizza; free ad-

vertising. Through a big clean window, you can
see the salesperson. He's really the cook, but he's
having so much fun flipping the dough around
that he does a great job of selling while he flips;
you think that pizza must be good. The people
who own the store know that eating pizza should
be a happy event (you wouldn't eat pizza if you
were depressed), and they've made a happy
store where everything works toward selling
pizza.

I try to do the same thing when I'm selling
my cookies. I'm already there, in my uniform,
which spells *Girl Scout* to the customers walking
by. The second year I was selling my uncle made
me my first cookie signs, which told the customers what I was doing there. One said, *Selling
Cookies, I'm Selling Cookies;* the other one said,
*Help Your Lincoln Towers Girl Scout by Buying
Cookies.* This sign was particularly good because
it was community-minded.

That's still not enough. It takes a lot to get
people's attention. So I sort of call out: "Great
Girl Scout cookies for sale." But I don't like re-
peating the same thing five times in a row. It's
boring. I try to think of as many different things
to say as possible: "Great Girl Scout cookies for
sale," "Help the Girl Scouts by ordering cookies," or my favorite, "Great cookies for a great
cause." Phew. I've now got their attention.
That's half the battle. (The other half is what you
say when you've "got" them, but we'll get to that
in the next chapter.)

You get your customers one by one, like an

You get your customers one by one, like an add-a-pearl necklace, and keeping each customer is as important to you as each pearl is to the necklace.

add-a-pearl necklace—and keeping each customer is as important to you as each pearl is to
the necklace, or as important as each vote is to
a politician. When I was first selling cookies, I got
really excited every time anybody bought a box.
I still get a feeling of satisfaction from each sale,
but it's a little different now. I keep thinking
ahead: How do I find more customers? Which
brings me to another of my rules of selling: You
don't know who your customers are until they're
your customers, until you sell and sell and sell.

And you can't sell and sell and sell unless you
take risks. I don't believe in luck; I believe that
luck is taking risks that turn out to be worth
taking.

Going into Potamkin Cadillac that first time
was a risk; I didn't know what I was getting into.
On a multiple-choice test, if I know that two
answers are wrong and don't know which of the
other two is right, guessing the right one is a risk.
Getting married is a risk, too, and so is every sale
you try to make for the first time. Writing this
book is a risk. So why take a risk? Because if you
don't, you'll never accomplish anything.

Sales risks are a little bit easier to take than
some other kinds, because what you're risking is
rejection—and rejection is something everyone
in sales has to learn to live with anyway. You'll
be rejected some of the time, risks or no risks.
Besides, in sales you can think through the risk
ahead of time.

For example, when I'm selling cookies in the
lobbies, sometimes I see strangers come in;

they're announced by the doorman. I know
these people don't live in the building—but that
doesn't mean they can't be my customers. But
they're somebody else's friends, and if they complain to their friends about me, I'll lose my
neighbors as customers, which is the last thing I
want to happen. So what I do is greet them and
ask if they want to buy cookies; I'm always careful to tell them the cookies won't be delivered
for a few weeks. "But I live in Alaska," they
might say. So I say: "Well, would you like to buy
a box as a gift for the friends you're visiting and
when they come I'll deliver them as a present
from you?" That was a new approach for me—
a risk that's been worth taking every year since.

The point in sales is always to follow the Girl
Scout motto, "Be prepared." See business when
it's there. Look at everyone and think, "Is this a
customer? How do I make this person buy?"

I missed a chance once to sell cookies to
Merlin Olsen, the football star who used to play
Father Murphy on the TV series. Now he's a
sports commentator. I still get mad that I
missed my chance to sell cookies to Father
Murphy! I was at an IBM convention, waiting
backstage; I was going to be doing a skit with
the president of one of the divisions. There was
another man waiting there, too, to go on before
me. The light was dim because the convention
was already going on, and he said "Hi," then I
said "Hi," and then I realized it was Merlin
Olsen. I couldn't believe it! I told him about my
cookies, then I realized I didn't have any to sell

him. I know he got to taste them because they were serving them as refreshments at the convention, but still. . . . Later on he sent me his picture, which I still have, but it would have been fun to sell him a box; I think he would have picked the mints.

Okay, you've got your customers all lined up in your mind; now you have a clientele. But the funny thing is that the more customers you have, the more time you have. For example, once I had been selling in the lobbies for awhile, both my customers and I knew what was going on: I'd sell and they'd buy. I didn't have to explain the cookies every time; they already knew about the cookies from the years before. And when a customer says, "Definitely the shortbreads again this year," my selling time is cut in half. So I have more time to find new customers.

I knew from my experience at Potamkin Cadillac that business places were good for selling cookies. But how to find more businesses? You can't just walk into General Motors and say, "Excuse me, I'm here to sell cookies!"

Start to build business by looking at your life, whether you're selling cars, computers, or cookies. The more people you know (more on this later), the more customers you know. I've been branching out since my second year of selling. I found Potamkin by taking a chance. But my aunt and I began organizing a real campaign that second year, too.

For example, my Uncle Walter is very involved with the West Side Republican Club: I
sold fifty boxes there when I was seven. (Too bad
my aunt's not a Democrat!) But Aunt Meredith
used to bowl at Beacon Lanes: twenty boxes. My
mother and my aunt get their hair done all the
time at the same hairdresser's and the people
there *love* cookies. . . . We go to the Fifth Avenue
Presbyterian Church. . . . I go to school. . . . The
more I get involved with people, the more I sell.

After the first couple of years, I began to get
more business from my conventions. One person
would let me come to sell at an office, and I'd go
back every year. The best thing about satisfied
customers is that they lead you to more satisfied
customers, so friends I made at a certain office
would recommend me to people at other offices,
and on and on. Occasionally, a company would
call the Girl Scouts and invite a Girl Scout over
to sell, and sometimes they would recommend
me. I also sell at conventions; my aunt and I have
been known to carry dozens of boxes of cookies
onto a plane with us. Last year, Random House
decided to do this book; I went around to two of
the floors there and sold eighty boxes (plus a few
raffle tickets) in two hours. The more you're selling the more fun you have—so on to the "se-
crets" of selling and selling and selling.

CHAPTER 5

OPENING
AND
CLOSING

To me, the opening is the hardest part of making a sale. I have only a second to figure out what kind of customer I have here: Does he hate cookies? Is she in a hurry? Would this one care about helping out the Girl Scouts? Should I recommend the chocolate mints to that one? Is this couple on a diet? At the same time the customer is trying to figure me out. What is this kid doing here? Does she care about *me* or is she just trying to sell to get famous? Will the cookies really come? Are they any good? Can I trust her? And

To sell you have to plunge right in, remember everything you know about your product and do your best to make your sale.

this is only to sell a simple box of cookies! What if I were trying to sell somebody a camper?

Selling—some for the good of humankind, some for the bad—has been going on for centuries. There used to be merchant ships and spice ships, but people also sold slaves and opium. Sales must be one of the oldest professions. In most cases I think the process works—the customer benefits and the salesperson does, too. But there have always been other cases when the salesperson cheats the customer, like one of those offers that's "too good to be true." (How do you think the Indians felt when they sold the island of Manhattan for twenty-four dollars?) People know that salespeople are making their living by taking other people's money; that's why they are a little suspicious. But buying and selling are natural parts of living, and people understand that, too. And honest people, especially honest salespeople, always do better in the end.

To sell you have to plunge right in, remember your manners and everything you know about your product and do your best to make your sale. You can't start by thinking about everything that could go wrong. You also can't think, "I have to stick to a certain strategy"; you have to be flexible. And you can't start by thinking that selling is all fun; it's work, too, hard work.

"May I help you?" "Is there something special you'd like to see?" "Would you like to try that dress on?" "Could I show you how this computer works?" When you're selling in a store, to a stranger, there aren't a whole lot of openings that will be original. (That's why how you present yourself—neatness, cheerfulness, etc.— counts so much: it sets you apart.) You wouldn't want to sell like crazy to someone who just dropped in to buy a bar of soap; they'd definitely think you were strange! But you would spend a little more time getting to know someone who might want to buy a car from you. A car costs more, and the buyer needs to trust you a *lot* before you even start talking about why Fords are better.

When I sell my cookies, I have different openings for each situation. If I'm selling in my apartment complex, I'm wearing my uniform, I have my sign, and I already know a lot of my neighbors. And by now, after all these years, my neighbors know why I'm there; I'm as familiar as Santa Claus at Christmas. So the more personal the approach the better.

I try to remember as many names as I can so that I can call my customer Mr. Gray or Mrs. Johnson. If I really know a person well, I can say, "How is Lavinia? Is her cold better?" then from there, suggest that Lavinia might like some cookies. If Lavinia is having a birthday party, I suggest it might be nice to serve cookies, perhaps along with pretzels and popcorn and peanuts, before serving the cake. "Oh, you're going away? How about bringing the hosts some cookies as a house gift?" I lead in like that. When I'm selling to my neighbors, I'm selling to my friends.

Selling in offices is for me a slightly different situation. Many times people will be sitting in their offices, and they look at me as if they're seeing things: *What* is this *Girl Scout* doing here? I wait at the door until I get the person's attention before I go in. And then I introduce myself, "Hi, I'm Markita Andrews, and I'm here selling Girl Scout cookies. . . ." I have to be quick —business people always seem busy with papers and I know I'm busy, too. I usually have only one afternoon to sell to an entire office. But not too quick. Sometimes I'm the only Girl Scout the people in offices have ever met, and I want to make a good impression. Besides, the customers want to feel that you have all the time in the world, just for them. We all want to feel that way when we're on the buying end.

When I first began selling cookies, my aunt helped me with ideas on what to say. She's had a million different kinds of jobs (she even sold once, door to door) and she knows a lot about business, so she was amazingly helpful. But she wanted me to learn to answer the questions myself, so I began to see that when you're selling cookies, or anything else, people almost always ask more or less the same questions and you have to have your answers ready. This is where selling begins to get creative.

I could tell you in my sleep the questions people ask about Girl Scout cookies: What are the best-sellers? What kind is your favorite? How much are they? How many kinds do you have? Do you have the original kind of Girl Scout cookies? Haven't they gone up since last year? (No, they've been the same price for the past three years—the best buy in town!) It does get nerve-wracking, the same questions over and over.

Now that I know these questions by heart, I try to answer them before the customer even asks them. ("The mints are the best sellers, but my favorites are . . .") There's a commercial on the radio that has the slogan, "An educated consumer is our best customer," and I think that means that the customer should know as much about the product as possible in order to decide what to buy. That's part of the seller's job, to educate. So maybe that makes me Professor of Cookies!

What's fun is to do the customers' thinking for them. A customer might be thinking, "Cookies? What will I do with cookies? But maybe I should buy some anyway; it's for a good cause." That's great for me: I can tell them about the mints, how they're good for after dinner, or just to set around during a party. Hotels sometimes put them on beds at bedtime—perhaps you could offer a few to guests late at night. Mints can be served by themselves or on the side when you're serving something else. When I get involved with a customer, I can understand the problem he or she is having with my product— and usually I can solve it.

On a diet? Our shortbreads have only

twenty-four calories each. Don't like crunchy
cookies? Our chocolate chips can be warmed in
the microwave for "home-style softness." One
child likes vanilla and another one chocolate?
How about mixed cookies, a box with half of
each? Not going to be home much? That's okay,
you can freeze the cookies for later. Tired of the
same old cookies? Try my favorites, these amazing cookies with coconut and caramel and if you
don't like them you can give them away to
friends. Concerned about health? Our cookies
contain no preservatives and no artificial color-
ing. You keep kosher? That's great—our cookies
are kosher!

You have to think about the *customer* no
matter what the business, not just with cookies.
It's your job to help the customer with ideas. Say
you work in a bookstore, it's winter and it's about
to snow. Bring out your winter sign! Set out a
special winter table full of books! What can people do during a snowstorm? Cook, do needle-
craft, read a spooky novel under the bed covers,
think ahead to summer sailing or gardening,
maybe there's a book on weather. Snowstorm
. . . winter . . . reading: You can come up with a
million ideas for them.

Or, say you work in a bike shop and somebody comes in thinking, "Do I want a bike or
not?" You can be ready for every question. Main-
tenance? You sell pumps. How to carry things?
Your special baskets. Where to go? Give out free
maps of park bike trails. Is it dangerous? Here's
a helmet. Show pictures of people having a great

time on bikes, maybe a biking video. You like
your bikes, you like your customers: You'll have
a great time putting them all together. The more
fun selling is for you, the more fun buying will be
for the customer.

During the sale my mind is always on the *sale*
—but there are a few things that I keep in the
back of my mind, too, things you should just remember automatically. Yawning, for example.
When you have to yawn you have to yawn, that's
all there is to it. I'm a person who yawns a lot.
But I make a point of yawning between customers. That way, no one sees me yawn.

It's also important to remember to be polite
to *everybody,* customer or not. I was once in a
store and the saleswoman was rude, not to me
but to another customer who was asking a lot of
questions. The customer was pretty rude, too.
(You do run into a certain amount of rudeness
when you're selling, but if you're polite it dis-
courages rudeness from others.) Finally, the customer left the store and it was my turn. The
saleswoman turned to me and was really nice.
But I had already seen her being rude—and
even when she was nice to me all I could remember was that she had been rude earlier. I didn't
buy anything and I never went back to the store.
The rude customer probably never went back
either. So she lost two customers, plus all the
other people we *both* might have told about her
store! Every time you lose a customer you could
really be losing many, many more.

My uncle says that if people you'd like to sell

to don't have a lot of money or seem to have a lot of money, you should be as kind and considerate as you can because someday, when they do have the money, they'll remember you and come back. If you weren't helpful, they won't. So every customer counts, even, in a funny way, if they don't buy.

Of course, it's always better if they *do* buy. So you can't just chat forever; you have to ask for that order.

Switching subjects (let's say from Lavinia's birthday party to whether Lavinia's mom wants cookies or not) and reaching the moment of truth—the order, that is—can also be tricky. But you're there to make your sale, not to talk all day about Lavinia. You can't be too shy about it.

It helps if there are lots of other customers around because the customer you're talking to will see that you're busy and get right down to ordering. (Also, if there are lots of customers right there, people will think: "I'd *better* buy cookies; all these other people are buying them and I'd be missing out if I didn't." It's exciting to be part of a crowd of buyers.)

But what if it's a slow day or if I'm in an office with one person who wants to keep on chatting all day? You can't switch from being *too* friendly to being *too* businesslike at the end; the customer will think, "What happened?" Selling is selling, and chatting is chatting. I chat, but not the same way I would chat if I were talking about Lavinia's birthday party on the elevator or anywhere I wasn't selling. I always keep to the subject of cookies, coming back to cookies every sentence or two. I don't want to get distracted and I don't want the customer to get distracted. If you don't keep talking about cookies, you'll end up talking about party hats, and you'll never get back on track.

This isn't rude. This is professional. When I want to close, I'll pull out my order form. Just as you lead into the sale, you can lead out when it comes time for the order. "Last year when Lavinia was having her birthday, we didn't have such-and-such cookies. Maybe it would be fun to try them this year." Or, "That's amazing, that you have never heard of Girl Scout cookies. See, here's a picture of all the different kinds we have." Or, "Yes, I do want to sell when I grow up, but I'm not sure what yet. But first I want to sell you some cookies!" The point is not to sneak into the sale. What you want instead is for the customer to say, "Yes, please, I'd love to buy some cookies from you!"

"I'll take one box." *ONE BOX????* Well, one box is always better than no box, and sometimes you'll be very happy with that one box. But one box isn't exactly selling and selling and selling. So here you thought you were at the end of the sale, and maybe you haven't even begun yet to sell and sell and sell. . . .

CHAPTER 6

SELLING
AND
THE
FIVE
SENSES

Banging, drums, drums, drums, and screech-
ing. If a store is playing rock music, some people
will go inside to see what's there—but a lot of
people won't bother just because the music is too
noisy. Seeing, hearing, tasting, touching, smelling. The five senses are what get people interested—think of the phrase "follow your nose"—
and if you make the most of your five senses
(along with your extra "secret" senses) when
you're selling whatever you're selling, then the
customer will not be able to resist seeing, hear-

ing, tasting, touching, or smelling your product —and buying it.

The first year I took orders for Girl Scout cookies, I had never even tasted them. If people asked me, "Are they good?" I had to say, "I don't know; I've never tasted them." That's not a very good answer for a salesperson to give. Cookies are mainly *taste*, so once I had tasted them (and I mean *all* the different kinds, believe me), I was better at selling them. I stopped talking about *boxes* to my customers. I always talked about *cookies* instead. Boxes don't make your mouth water; cookies do! So now I try to use as many of the senses as I can when I sell.

There are pictures of all the cookies on our order forms; you can *see* the cookies before you buy them. I know that helps, but sometimes I add a little: "You could serve the mints in a pretty silver dish at your next dinner party." You can just see how elegant that would be! Or smelling: "You open the box and you can just smell the peanut butter. . . ." Hearing: "This kind is so crunchy. . . ." Touching: "These are bumpy cookies, and you have to lick the chocolate off your fingers after you eat them. . . ." But with cookies, taste is the main thing. "Chewy, buttery, chocolate-y, lemon-y—pralines, coconut" and on and on. I get hungry just talking about cookies—and I want to make my customers hungry, too.

When you go into a store to buy a dress, you can see everything about it before you buy. You can see how it looks, how it's made; you can really think about whether you need it and will wear it a lot. But the funny thing about selling, even selling cookies, is that many times you're selling things that aren't even *there,* or else things you can't be sure in advance your customers will like. People buy computers before they know how to work them, or food before they've tasted it, or books before they know they'll enjoy them. I sell my cookies weeks before I deliver them. So selling is really two things: describing and convincing. And you can use the five senses to do both.

Let's say you're a travel agent, and you're trying to sell a special deal for a trip to Hawaii. (I went to Hawaii once to give a speech for Lotus Development Corporation; I *loved* it!) Your customers will have to pay the money before they go, before they know if they're going to have a good time. So you have to describe the trip to them, and then make them want to go.

To make them see Hawaii: posters, pictures, brochures—better still, show them a video of what it's like in Hawaii. Use words like "beach" instead of "package deal." Fill your office with flowers that *smell* like Hawaii. Play Hawaiian music. Maybe have a few Hawaiian souvenirs around so they can hold them and see what they can buy when they get there. Tell them about a Hawaiian restaurant they might want to try, so they'll know what kind of food they'll be able to have when they go. Sell Hawaii!

The dress salesperson doesn't have to tell you the dress is red; you're in the dressing room, wearing the dress, and you can see perfectly well that it's red. She doesn't have to describe; her job is to convince. Maybe she can't use all five senses to sell (how do you taste a dress?), but she can still be a great salesperson.

She can be helpful, for example, by getting you different colors or sizes or bringing you more outfits to try on; that makes shopping fun for you and not a chore—you'll want to buy a dress from her. She can find out what you like to do. If you're going to a party, she can make you see yourself in the dress *at that party,* not just in the dressing room. She can bring you belts and scarves to go with the dress, so you look even prettier. And she can use other senses in her store: nice music, pretty dressing rooms, maybe free perfume to try on with the clothes. . . .

Or, pretend you're selling trumpets. With trumpets, hearing is the main thing—but not the only thing. The customers also have to be able to *see* themselves as trumpet players; that's your job. Plus people don't just drop into a store to buy a trumpet; they take a lot of time to decide. Maybe they're thinking, "Should I learn to play the trumpet or the violin?" You might have to sell the *idea* of trumpets before you can sell *a* trumpet.

You can learn trumpet history and show with a picture guide how trumpets used to look. Maybe you could have pictures around of great trumpet players. Play cassettes of how a bad trumpet sounds, then how much better a good one (yours!) plays. Trumpet music should

be your background music at all times. You can
show how they look before they're all shined
up, then shine one yourself (with your cleaning
equipment) to show how it's done. Keep sheet
music around for trumpet players at all levels.
Maybe they could "try on" a trumpet and look
at themselves in the mirror. And maybe they'll
see there the greatest trumpet player of all
time!

When you start thinking about the senses, it's
easier to know how to sell your product. Just
think of how many things sell by smell: perfumes
(I love those scratch-'n-sniff ads), bakeries, ham-
burger restaurants, new cars, leather shoes,
flowers, all kinds of things. Let the customer
touch whenever possible. (If I'm in a store buying socks, I'll buy the ones that are not all pack-
aged up. I like to touch.) Is there a sample they
can taste? What do you want them to hear when
you're selling? And how much can they see?
(There's a health food store near where I live.
They can't show "health," but there's a picture
of a healthy-looking person on practically every
package.)

And whatever the customers can't see, hear,
taste, touch or smell right there—tell them
about it in words! You can make them see, hear,
taste, touch, and smell just by talking. . . .

With the five senses, you're thinking about
the customer. Your other, "secret" selling senses
(say *that* five times fast) are more to help *you*
when you're selling; use them all the time and
your customers will know that you're a kind and

Use *all* your senses to sell,
including your "secret" ones
—your intuition,
your sense of humor
and your common sense.

understanding salesperson, and a good and thoughtful "regular" person, too.

To me, intuition in selling—that's the first secret sense—is what you know about a person before he or she tells you a thing. For example, if you can tell that somebody is in a hurry, you'll sell differently—faster, for one thing. When I'm selling cookies in the lobbies, I prefer to talk to people on their way home, not on their way out when they're almost always in a rush. Sometimes they're in a hurry anyway, so either I'll try to speed things up or get their phone number and tell them I'll call later for their order. (And I do call later.)

For some reason, I can sell more cookies to women than I can to men. Women seem more willing to take a little extra time (which also makes us good salespeople!) or maybe women just know more about the Girl Scouts. My intuition tells me to be brisker with men, which I try to do. But don't think that men can get away with not buying. When William Geist was writing an article about me last year for the *New York Times*, we caught a guy trying the "oldest line in the book": He told me his wife had already bought cookies. Wrong. Aunt Meredith and I checked. And then called up his wife for her order. (He was in the article, so I don't think he'll try that one again. Will you, Mr. X?)

Intuition also tells me to speak more slowly and use the pictures more when I'm selling to someone who doesn't speak English well; to speak up when I'm selling to someone who is older. And to be especially cheerful with people who are grumpy or sad. I just say, "Excuse me, we have great cookies for sale and I know it would make you feel good to buy some—when they come you'll be in for a surprise!" Girl Scout cookies are supposed to make people happy, and I think they do.

It's also intuition that tells me when to stop, when I'm being too persistent. (I know I've made mistakes that way.) It's hard to know, until after I've done it, when I'm being too persistent. Often people will say, "One box," and when I've given them more ideas, they'll change their order to more. If I don't go after them, I'll lose. those extra sales. But if I go after them too hard, then people won't buy from me. They'll think, "All she does is ask and ask for more; she's never happy with what she gets." But how do you tell when to stop? By going slowly when you're asking for more and stopping the very first second the customer seems impatient. By intuition.

Sometimes intuition will tell you to stop working for the day, maybe even before you've met your goals, just because everything is going wrong and you're having trouble getting your act together. Or, your intuition might tell you to keep going a little longer, even if you have met your goals—or, to try something a little bit different. And intuition is great for telling when friends need cheering up or when you'd better stop being difficult. (My uncle says that teenagers are people who do and say exactly the opposite of what they're supposed to do and say, but even teenagers have intuition.) Listen to your intuition. It works best with your second secret selling sense: your sense of humor.

I don't think Girl Scout cookies are very funny, but some people do—so I have to have a sense of humor about them, and also about myself. Your sense of humor keeps you going, no matter what you're doing.

When I was speaking that time before the Million Dollar Roundtable, I was up on the stage and they asked me to go through rules you should follow when you're selling. So I went through them. "One," I said, "you should know your product. . . . Two, you should go where the customers are. . . . Three, you should know your product. . . ." Then I said something like, "Wait. Stop. No, no, no, no, no!" It's all on tape, full color, and you can see me with my hands over my face. Everybody's laughing (and Radio City Music Hall holds a *lot* of people)—me, too.

Not everyone is going to say yes; that's rejection. Laughing at myself (and at them, too, but only to myself) helps me to be able to take it. And I've learned that Girl Scout cookies aren't the most serious thing in the world. But the best thing is to be able to laugh with a customer; a sense of humor on both sides brings people together.

You would think that everyone in the world is on a diet—a lot of people groan when they hear *cookies,* then complain about how they can't eat them because of their diet. Then I always tell them about the shortbreads (only twenty-four calories, as you now know), about freezing the cookies (a lot of people like them frozen), about how everyone needs a little sweetness after a hard day's work, about how the proceeds go to a great cause. . . . Somehow, the subjects of dieting and cookies get people laughing. And the dieters usually say, "Oh, all *right.*" They feel good because they tried to say no; I feel good because they said yes. (They also feel good because they're getting cookies after all.) We've played a game—and had fun! A sense of humor will keep your product, and you, from being boring. And that leaves just one "secret" sense.

Common sense is your third secret sense. As Uncle Walter would say: You have it. Use it.

CHAPTER 7

DON'T
BE
AN
OSTRICH

I hate avocados. Tomatoes, peppers, fine, I could sell those. But could I sell avocados? Even if I don't like them?

Other questions: Am I selling something I believe in and care about? Something I'm proud of? Do I understand my product? When I'm selling cookies, I'm proud to be a Girl Scout. I believe in the cookies and I believe in the cause. I don't think you can be what I call an ostrich salesperson: Your head buried in the sand, selling something that "feels" wrong or doesn't make sense to you.

My cookies make sense to me. You have to look at your product or your job, and then at the world around you: Does it all fit together? Does it fit into what I call the chain reaction of selling?

Some people—say they're in Minnesota—invent a product, then they make it in a factory. Next, other people go around the country to sell it to stores. Then the people in the stores sell it to the consumers. (There may be ads for it, too.) The consumers take it home, supposedly to use it, wear it, eat it, whatever. But maybe the people in Minnesota aren't actually sure about what people in New Hampshire really want; maybe they're just having fun inventing products. So you can't think only about *your* part of the chain: You have to see the *whole* chain. Or else you'll be an ostrich salesperson.

There's a whole chain reaction with my cookies, too. There are the Girl Scouts of the USA, the Girl Scout Council of Greater New York, plus 335 more local Girl Scout councils. Think how many Girl Scout councils there are all over the country! There's a cookie chairwoman for New York City every year, and I assume there's one for every other city, too. There are the people who make the cookies, the people who make the boxes, the people who deliver the cookies. Not to mention the Girl Scouts who sell the cookies, the people who buy the cookies, and all the others I can't even think of. So when one Girl Scout (me!) sells cookies, she's part of the whole big chain.

Don't be an ostrich:
selling is one step in
a chain, a people chain.

Selling is like the biggest chain letter in the world.

People who sell horses and buggies can't pretend there are no cars. That's being an ostrich. They would have to think about other ways horses and buggies can fit into the world—maybe to drive tourists through parks for fun, the way they're used in Central Park in New York. Otherwise you'd have people saying, "What are you talking about, a horse and buggy? I drive a Chevy!"

If you're selling candles, you shouldn't forget that lightbulbs are pretty popular these days. Why make a special display of snowboots on a summer day? You have to look and see what's going on in the world, then look at your product: *Where* does it fit in? For example, I wouldn't try to sell Girl Scout cookies in a bakery. Selling is looking around!

Back to avocados (though I'd really rather skip avocados). Avocados, for instance, fit right in; people are eating a lot of them these days. And even though I don't like them myself, yes, I think I could sell them. First of all, I wouldn't be selling just avocados. They're part of a chain of selling: What would a vegetable store be without avocados? Any store that sells avocados sells other things, too, so I wouldn't be spending all my time with avocados. Second, a lot of customers would come in and just buy avocados—no questions asked. I wouldn't have to say one way or another how I felt about them, except maybe to say how fresh they were that day.

And third, if people did ask me, "What are these disgusting-looking things?" I could answer honestly: "Avocados. I don't like them personally, but a lot of people do. You can cut them into strips and put them in salads. Or, make guacamole by mushing them up. Or, you can put them on your face, have a facial with them. They're not expensive; why not give one a try?" I could even have avocado recipes on hand. With avocados, my personal beliefs would not be on the line, just my tastebuds. If I refused to sell avocados, with all that protein, I'd be an ostrich. So I bet I could sell a lot, and my customers would appreciate my honesty. (A different situation would be selling guns, something I would never do, because I could never feel comfortable with them.)

Buyers do, and should, think about how much salespeople know about what they're trying to sell. Whether it's a tree, a house or a TV set, the seller should know all about the price, the different kinds, the features it comes with—and how it fits into the world.

With an avocado you could say, "Why not give it a try?" You can't say that to a customer thinking of buying a house. If you're selling a house, you're selling the neighborhood and the neighbors, the churches, schools and stores, nearby activities, the scenery, the crime rate, the weather, the fair price, and every other little detail you can think of about the house itself. If you're selling houses, you probably live nearby and know the neighborhood. But the better you know it, the more houses you'll sell. The customer will see that you are really trying to help, not just trying to make the sale and get it over with. If you understand the chain, you won't be an ostrich.

To me, one of the great things about being a salesperson is that the job *makes* you look around and learn new things all the time. I don't think I would like sitting in the same office every single day with the same people. When you're a salesperson, you're on the move and you can see new people each day. That works to your advantage when you're selling (you keep selling more and more), and it also makes you a more interesting person. If you let it.

If you're selling cars, let's say, and you absolutely *adore* cars, you have to be careful to avoid becoming an ostrich car salesperson. You can't just think about cars, engines, and transmissions, waiting for customers to walk in the door to buy cars from you. Cars are not the only point. What do you do with cars? You can put tape decks in them; you can take them to the beach; you can go on trips. You can drive around with your friends. Or, you can stay in the garage with your engines and transmissions. Guess which will be more fun and better for sales? The lesson is: Get out in the world! See what your product can do! Get new ideas!

My really good teachers know this. They're selling their subjects, remember, and what they'll do is show us movies of the things we're studying or take us places to show us subjects in action. They know that subjects don't exist only in books. Earlier I mentioned Mrs. Chapin, who teaches history and geography. Every spring she takes kids to places like India or Israel—history and geography come alive. Becky, my editor, told me about a science teacher she once had who would take her classes out to West Texas every year to teach them about biology and ecology. School is for the world, not just for the classroom.

A really nice shoe salesman my mother and I met knew this, too. We were buying shoes for me, and it was almost cookie season. I said I needed shoes that would be comfortable to stand in for hours on end. (That's another thing. Always take care of your feet.) Then my mother told him about my cookie selling. He was really interested, asked lots of questions. And he really cared that I had the right kind of shoes: "These would be good cookie shoes." You see, his head wasn't buried in the shoes he was selling. At the end, as one seller to another, he gave me a discount and even a free pair of socks. He was so nice. I always buy my shoes from him now—and he always buys Girl Scout cookies from me!

The thing is, look at your product and picture in your mind how the customer would look using it. This is why I suggest cookies as dessert for dinner parties. I always imagine a white tablecloth and the customer's very best china. . . .

The people who make Cabbage Patch dolls practically write plays about the dolls; they definitely see their dolls out in the world. They come in every possible way the customer might like to have them—black, white, twins. You can get glasses for them, or a "first tooth." Someone at camp told me they even make Cabbage Patch coffins for dolls that get ripped up by pets. The Cabbage Patch kids seem so lifelike. You feel that the company *loves* them—you have to love them, too. They're not just dolls like the others that sit on shelves in stores.

Same thing with companies that welcome cards and letters or have hotlines for your questions: These are the companies that make the selling process more personal. They understand the chain reaction; they're not ostriches. (I try to be personal, too, when I'm selling cookies—and even when I'm not. If a neighbor asks me to go to the store as a favor and I can do it, I will. That's part of being a Girl Scout—or a person—too. Or, when I'm babysitting, I try to do a little bit extra, cleaning up or reading lots of stories to the children. So I get paid more than some babysitters do. Extra touches, in selling or anything else, *do* make a difference.)

And then think not about *your* taste, but your customer's. For example, my favorite Girl Scout cookies are made with coconut, caramel, and chocolate—but which kind do I sell the most of? Mints. "Those might be fine for *you*," customers probably think, "but give me mints any day." I have to respect their taste.

On the other hand, the cookies that sell second best are the Samoas—*my* favorites. Which means that when people trust a salesperson, they believe the salesperson knows the product and they are willing to listen to the advice of an expert. That's where you come in. If you're not an ostrich, you'll be able to give them the whole picture; you'll get to express your tastes when selling.

But to express your tastes first you have to know what they are. So even when you're not selling, it's important not to be an ostrich in life. A small example is recently when I had a chance to have lobster for dinner—the real thing, claws and all. I had had lobster before, but cut up and out of the shell: a different matter. So I tried it, and liked it! Every new thing you do makes you a changed person. (I am still an ostrich when it comes to squid, though—and avocados!)

There are so many ways to join in the world, not be an ostrich. I think it's important to start when you're young, and there are so many things that kids can do today: singing, dancing, playing in a band, spelling bees, selling, starting a street-lot garden. Aunt Meredith says that if you want to get something done, ask the busiest person you know to do it. She has a million activities all going on at once; she and Uncle Walter are the busiest people I know. They've always taught me that it's important to be involved in your community.

Uncle Walter, for example, was a delegate to the Republican National Convention in 1980; when my Aunt Meredith was a delegate four years later, guess who got to go? Me! And Aunt Meredith takes me along to the local Republican

Club sometimes, so I help out with phones, etc.; I also have a souvenir pen and photo from First Lady Nancy Reagan. We do things for our church, for the Girl Scouts—for good causes and for fun. One thing leads to another. For example, because of my cookies, I was invited by Mayor Koch to lead the Pledge of Allegiance along with a Boy Scout during the ceremony at City Hall to welcome home the hostages from Iran. I'll never forget that.

What was also fun for me was when Aunt Meredith and Uncle Walter helped to plant flowers along the strips of grass in the middle of Broadway near where we live. They let me come along to help. Talk about a chain reaction: Everyone appreciated the flowers and the effort it took. There were pretty things to look at, less litter; everyone in the neighborhood and the people who come there to shop could enjoy the benefits. For me it was great. I met a lot of new people, so when cookie time came 'round the next year—more customers for my cookies!

CHAPTER 8

THE
DOWN
SIDE
OF
SELLING

Death, failure, rejection, getting fired or flunking, being laughed at, making some terrible mistake. I'm afraid of all these things (except being fired, because I don't have a job yet); I think everybody is. In a way, it would be a bit strange *not* to be afraid of things like these—because many of them will happen to all of us at one time or another. You have to be philosophical.

On top of the fears we all have, everyone has private fears, too. I once saw a really creepy movie where these creatures lived in the basement of a house and could turn off the lights and go up chimneys—to kill people. Only the repairman knew about them. He was warning the man who lived in the house that the creatures were going to kill the owner's wife, and then they both realized that the wife was alone in the house. . . . I was really little when I saw the movie, but I still remember it sometimes if I'm home alone studying or if I hear any odd noises. That's not my main fear—I don't even have a chimney— but it's just one of those little fears that can get to you.

It's possible that someone can be really smart, fun, pretty, but imagine that she's not smart, or that she's ugly, or fat. Some people who should have all the confidence in the world just don't have it; they're shy instead, worried all the time that they're not good enough. A bad self-image is a different kind of private fear; if you look at everything from this I'm-not-good-enough perspective, the world will never be a very attractive place to you.

Your self-image is not what you seem like to others but what you feel like inside. Just because the world thinks you're okay doesn't mean that *you* think you're okay, too. That's too bad: Most people really are smart and kind, but what counts more is that they believe it. It's harder to believe it than to *know* it from what others tell you. Someone can say to you, "You look so pretty today," and maybe you sort of believe him but look in the mirror yourself and think, "Ugly." You can know in your mind that your friend *might* be right but still not believe it in your heart. And in selling you need a good self-image: There are times when we all fail, get rejected, get laughed at, and make terrible mistakes.

It's funny how a good self-image can come and go. It happens to me. Selling cookies has given me a lot of confidence. After all, I've been at it since I was six. But then last year somebody at school said, "Markita, you've been in all the newspapers with your cookies. Why don't you sell to the class?" Self-image down the drain. I was so nervous; I didn't know if the people in my class would make fun of me or not. I kept postponing it, forgetting my order form, etc. Then one day a really nice girl in my class said, "*Today* Markita is going to sell us cookies." Okay, okay. So I did, and it was fine. But how do you get over fears like this?

I think you get over fears like this by *not* getting over fears like this, funny as that may sound.

I *had* to sell to my class; no way I could get out of it. But there was also no way I wasn't going to be afraid. I'll be afraid next year, too, if I have to do it again. In a way it makes me feel better to admit that I'm really shy about this or that. Shyness takes up a lot of energy, and being afraid of something can make you very tired. When you're caught in the trap of shyness, you have two choices: Am I going to use up the energy to get deeper in the trap or to get *out* of the trap. Out is always better. And so the cycle is first to admit to yourself that you're shy or afraid; then,

Doing what you're afraid of makes you feel *twice* as good—afterwards.

admit it to others—if that helps (often people will be gentler with you if you know you're nervous—they'll understand); finally, go ahead and do what you're afraid of, because, as my uncle always says, you'll have to do it sooner or later and you might as well get it over with!

Doing things that you're nervous about is like going to school with a cold. You know you'll get through it somehow, but it's *no fun*. The fun, the relief, comes when the cold goes away or when you've done what you were afraid of. Then you feel twice as good as usual.

You can also get used to certain fears. They may never go away entirely, but the more you do the thing you dread, the less scary it is. You can get used to a job, become less nervous as time goes on. Public speaking is like that, too; it's a little easier each time you do it. I remember my first speaking engagement. It was in Florida, and I was so excited about going to Florida that I almost forgot I had to give a speech until the time came. At that moment I would have given anything not to have gone to Florida! But I gave the speech (had no choice); when I give speeches now, I'm still nervous, but nothing like that first time. I'm getting used to it.

Same thing with nervousness about making a mistake—once you've made one, you find that you can live with it (have no choice!), awful as it may be. Everybody has fears, and everyone makes mistakes, too. Making a mistake is the worst feeling, and it doesn't help that every time you think about it later you get embarrassed all over again! The second or third year I was selling, for example, I misread on the order form an order for the people in a certain apartment; I think I had the right apartment number, wrong name. They owed me money, I thought, and it was an order for several boxes. Typical me, I kept calling and calling, and they kept saying they didn't owe me money and they hadn't ordered cookies. They got really mad. Everything got worse. By the time I realized my mistake they hated me; they wouldn't even listen to my apology.

To this day these people ignore me, and every time I see them I still feel terrible—but less terrible than I used to feel. Okay, I made a mistake, I tell myself. But was it a mistake that should have made them stay mad at me all these years? No. Learn from your mistakes, my uncle always says—and I've sure learned from this one. I double check names and apartments; I do it right away. Maybe I made that one mistake, but that one mistake prevented me from making that one mistake ever again, if that makes sense. Making mistakes, sad as it may sound, is a good way to become a better salesperson!

I've made other mistakes, too. The Girl Scouts prefer that the customer write down his own name and address on the order form or that you have an adult with you to do it so that there's less chance of making a mistake. A couple of times, when I was way too young to keep track of the orders, I thought, "Well, I'll just keep track of these orders myself. I can do it." The

Girl Scouts were right, I was wrong and it took Aunt Meredith and me hours to undo the damage. Another lesson learned. I've also learned that there's a time for TV and a time for homework, but it's not the *same* time. (True confessions.)

Stress—from fears, from pressure, from mistakes you do make and mistakes you think you might make—can also be a major problem in selling, school, anything you do. I see a lot of stress in the world around me; I feel it myself sometimes: I-can't-take-it-anymore pressure. You know the feeling, too. What if you were selling flowers, say, day in and day out. You'd reach a point where you'd want to say, "There are the daffodils, and here are the geraniums. Go get them yourself!"

Writers can get writer's block. Sellers can get seller's block; teachers can get teacher's block; carpenters can get carpenter's block; students, student's block. The English teacher I had last year must have had a lot of pressure on her. We're always doing essays, and she teaches eighth through eleventh grades. She must be constantly reading all these essays. How she does it I don't know, but even though she works hard, she never *seems* pressured. I wish I could be as calm.

There's always stress of some kind, whatever you're doing—even, believe it or not, selling cookies. There's one doorman who never wants me around selling or even delivering cookies; I don't know why. Sometimes I have to deliver cookies to someone who's only home when he's on duty—stress. Then there's one nosey lady who always, without fail, says to me, "Do you have permission to sell here? I'm calling the management." And I always say, "Yes, ma'am, I do have permission"; the doormen back me up, too. But it's still stressful. Once I asked a man I had never asked before if he wanted to buy some cookies; I was perfectly polite. He got practically hysterical: "Young lady I do *not* want to buy cookies!" Stress for me. For him, too, I would guess.

Rejection like that takes your confidence away faster than Superman can fly. You want to say, "Excuse me, I think I'll just go up to my bed now and cry." Maybe sometimes you have to do just that. Other times you have to let your private fears "talk" to you. When I get rejected, the person inside me thinks, "Well, they didn't buy cookies from me because they think I look terrible or they just don't like me," or something like that. You can guess how helpful that is.

There are two kinds of rejection. Some people are polite about it, "Thank you anyway, Markita, but I really can't buy any." That's fine with me. I thank them back, and it's almost as nice as it would have been if they *had* bought cookies. They don't hate me, I can see; they hate cookies!

Other people are mean about saying *no* rudely. I thank them, too, but there's no pleasure in it. I try to ask myself what's wrong with *them,* why they're going to so much trouble to make me feel awful. I can't blame myself every time

someone refuses to buy cookies. You have to accept rejection, but maybe you never get used to it, I don't know. You have to go on to the next person if you're going to continue to sell, that's all there is to it. The funny thing is that after a rejection I often make a great sale, sort of to get rid of the bad feeling of rejection. I want to make myself bounce back after someone says *no,* to say to myself, "See, I can do it after all!" If everyone said yes, selling wouldn't be selling, I suppose. And in a way, it's up to you whether you'll concentrate on the things that have gone right or the things that have gone wrong.

One blessing is that you can control the conversations you have with yourself.

A friend of mine who goes to my school is amazingly smart, energetic, cheerful. She always knew how to make everybody feel better. "What's wrong?" "Smile!" "Have a happy face!" She never seems down, or if she is, you can never tell. I think it makes her happy just cheering people up all the time, giving pep talks. And I think she really does cheer people up. I'm always be happy at least on the outside when I'm with her, because I don't want *her* to feel bad! (At least that takes my mind off *me!*)

I wish I had a tape of her to carry with me for those times when I need it. Instead, I kind of give pep talks to myself, or anyway try to. If something has gone wrong, if you've made a mistake, if you're feeling I-can't-take-it-anymore pressure, then it's time to have a little talk with yourself. And a good way to open the conversation is by simply saying to yourself, "Now, let's see what the problem is here."

You may find that the problem is not with your selling or your work at all. The problem may be with something else, and you're just taking it out on your work. It's good to figure that out right away, because it won't help to get mad at your job if you're really mad at your husband, mother, teacher, or congressman. I know that sometimes I'm in a bad mood when I'm selling and if I think about it, I can see that it's not the *selling* that's putting me in a bad mood; the selling is fine. What's putting me in a bad mood is missing a really good TV show or knowing that I have to do my chores after I finish selling. So instead of blaming selling, I can blame my bed for not being made—and all of a sudden selling seems like a big treat!

Another question to ask yourself is, "Just why am I working so hard?????" Are you working hard to win a prize or so that you can go on a trip? Think about the prize or trip and keep going; your reward is just around the corner. Are you working to compete with someone? Why would you do that? Are you trying to prove something to yourself or somebody else? Is that really necessary? Sort out the problem. Maybe you've set ridiculous goals and the answer is *not* to work so hard.

Sometimes to get the job done, you have to stop doing the job; that could be the problem. Maybe you're not seeing the forest for the trees, as my uncle would say. If all you're doing is selling and selling and selling, you won't know whether it's summer or winter, night or day. If selling is all you're thinking about, you'll forget that there's also a world outside—and that's not good. So how do you cure that?

To sell you have to take selling breaks. To study you have to take study breaks. People who work in offices take coffee breaks. (But too much caffeine is not good for you, so be careful.) Weekends are breaks from what you do all week. I know I sometimes have to *make* myself stop, just so I can make myself go back to the task. Take a break, take a walk, take a nap, have a snack, relax, do whatever you want—except sell. When I clean out my drawers (which, according to my mother and my aunt, is never often enough), I feel that my whole life is all of a sudden organized. Or, if you're not up to that, go to a movie or read a book. (I just read *A Separate Peace,* which I would recommend to anyone.) Have some fun in your life!

Then, after you've had that chat with yourself, turn to the people you love, your family, your friends. Don't they always cheer you up? Friends and family are like the backup services of your heart. And when you're ready to go back to selling, all that's left to think about are the backup services of your profession. . . .

CHAPTER 9

BACK-UP
—AND
FOLLOW-UP

Last year when I went to Potamkin Cadillac to sell cookies to my friend Mr. Potamkin, he said he would take twenty-five boxes. "Hmmm . . . ," I said to myself.

Mr. Potamkin has been buying cookies from me since I was seven, so I know him pretty well by now, at least in a cookie sense. He buys the cookies to give out in his cafeteria, I think, which is great. The reason I thought "Hmmm" when he said twenty-five boxes was that the year before last he bought seventy boxes. I wasn't sure if I should mention this to him or not, since he had other people in the room with him, and also I didn't want to sound as if I were complaining. Mr. Potamkin is one of my most loyal customers, and he has always been kind to me. Plus, I *wasn't* complaining; I just wanted to know if he knew that he was ordering less than usual. Sometimes customers have to be reminded of things.

So I took a chance, even in front of his business friends: "But you bought seventy boxes last year, Mr. Potamkin. Don't you want to beat what you bought last year?" They were all pretty amazed that I remembered an order for a whole year, and he said, "Okay, fifty boxes." That was fine for me, and it also showed him that I cared enough about him and about my job to remember his order all that time.

The point in selling is to make connections— and keep them. In a way this part of selling is the most fun; you get to thank all kinds of people for all they've done for you, and some people will even thank you back for all you've done for them! Back-up and follow-up, I call it. Follow-up will keep your connections to your customers, and back-up—short for back-up services—will keep you connected to the people who make it possible for you to sell in the first place.

The first rule of follow-up is remembering to write your thank-you notes. You can see that I haven't mentioned thank-you notes until the last chapter, just in the nick of time. That's the way I am in real life, too, unfortunately. I keep postponing them and postponing them, as my aunt

The first rule
of follow-up is
remembering to write
your thank-you notes.

will be the first to tell you. I mean to write them right away. "Yes, today is a fine day to write that thank-you note," I'll say, but you know how that goes. . . .

Aunt Meredith is right, though; I know why thank-you notes are important, and when I finally do get around to writing them, I feel terrific! Thank-you notes say that you're a person who really appreciates what another person has done for you. People will think, "How nice. She thought enough to write." And it's true, you did think enough to write. Don't *you* feel terrific when someone writes *you* a thank-you note???

There are a few people it makes me especially happy to sell to (and write thank-you notes to) every year, Mr. Potamkin for one. And Mr. Edelston, my friend from *Boardroom Reports,* has been wonderful to me practically my whole life. Every year he buys a *lot* of cookies from me. He told me he gives them to his daughter, who puts them into her backpack at college and gives them out to her friends. (This always makes me think of Johnny Appleseed!) Mr. Allen Seskin from AMS Consulting is also my friend, and every year he buys a *lot* of cookies, too. He lets me donate them to my church project, which gives food and clothing to people less fortunate than we are—buying cookies for a good cause to give to a good cause.

I always write thank-you notes to people who let me sell cookies at their companies and people who invite me to conventions. I'll always appreciate Mr. Frank Baiamonte of American Bankers

Insurance Group, for example, who was the first person ever to have me speak at a convention. (He lives in Florida and sometimes he sends me oranges, too!) I also get a lot of letters back from people I meet at conventions, thanking *me* for giving my speeches, which my aunt and I keep in scrapbooks. Thank-you notes can work both ways.

Notes of all kinds can really make a difference, as I learned by accident. The Girl Scouts provide us with these little blue forms that say something like, "We tried to deliver your cookies but you were out." They're really useful, because sometimes tracking people down to deliver their cookies is harder than finding people to sell them to. Well, last year I lost my forms, couldn't find them anywhere. Aunt Meredith and I had to write all the notes ourselves, and I'm talking about a *lot* of notes. It was worse than being grounded. But the surprise was that so many people came up to me to say, "How nice of you to write that note," which they never did with the blue forms. It goes to show you what a personal touch can do, and how much thank-you notes really mean to people. So you write yours, and I *promise* to be more prompt with mine.

If you're selling the *New York Times* at a newsstand every day, of course, you couldn't write a thank-you note to every single person who bought a paper from you every single day. That's ridiculous. I don't have time to write a thank-you note to every single person in my apartment complex either. (I have enough trouble writing them as it is.) But you just know somehow when a sale calls for a note. Guilt will set in—and guilt can get you going with those notes! Let your conscience be your guide.

But how do you thank your customers when you can't write a note? The first way is to say, "Thank you!" Every sale calls for a thank-you, that's all there is to it. The second way is just by remembering your customers—look at them, talk to them, try to memorize as much as you can about them, so the next time you see them you can say, "Hi! How did you like the cookies?" Or the dress, or the couch, or the computer? Someday they may want to buy another dress, couch, or computer—or they may have friends who do. And not just that—you don't want people to think you're some kind of a robot who can only talk about what she sells. People feel close to people, not to robots, so be a person, too! "Are you going on a nice summer vacation?" "Is your Christmas shopping done?" "Can you believe how much it rained yesterday?" "What a pretty outfit!" Chances are good that if you remember your customers, they'll come to remember you, too.

You can also thank your customers by phone —just a call to say thank you, or even simply leaving a message on the person's answering machine or with her secretary, can make a difference and show you care. A good salesperson is one whose sales never end! If I were a travel agent, I think I'd call up my customers after their trips to see if they had a good time. If I sold cars, I could call my customers up to remind them about tune-ups. When a friend gives me a referral or helps me out, I always call to say thank you. As my uncle says, common courtesy is pretty uncommon these days. People notice.

Another thing Uncle Walter always says is that common courtesy begins at home. This is where back-up services come in. Think of yourself, the salesperson, as being in the middle. On one side of you, lined up, are your customers; you already know about thanking them. On your other side are your back-up people. If you sell for a living, they're the people in your company, the people who do the shipping, the people who make the product, the list goes on and on. But if one thing goes wrong anywhere along the line, you're sunk. You won't be able to do your job.

When I think of back-up services, I think first of my Aunt Meredith, who has helped me with my cookies from day one. She's incredible. When I was little she would arrange everything so that I could be where I had to be to sell and come with me (because Brownies must be accompanied by an adult to sell). Now I try to do more of the organizing, but she's still there, still driving me places, accompanying me when I know I'll have a lot of money to handle, talking to the people who call about conventions, doing all she can. The best thing is that sometimes when I'm low I don't tell her, but I know she knows. (How does she know?) Maybe for you the person who does the most to help you is your husband or wife or best friend, and haven't you

Thank-yous go in
two directions—to
the customers who
buy from you, and to
the people who make
it possible for you to
sell, and sell,
and sell . . .

wondered, "How can I thank this person enough?"

I hope my aunt knows I'm grateful. I thank her, and this book is dedicated to her, and I make things for her at the Girl Scouts or camp. Dedicating this book to her is another thank-you, and I can thank her again right here! And thank my uncle, too, who makes me my signs and helps drive around and deliver cookies. . . . And my mother, who sometimes sits with me in the lobbies when I sell, who works so hard to support us —and who I know is proud of me. . . . And all my friends and relatives (and there are a *lot* of relatives to thank: My aunt and my mother had eight kids in their family, and you can't believe how many aunts and cousins and uncles I have!).

I was watching the news a couple of months ago and saw an interview with a man who owns a company that makes special shavers, who seemed like the nicest man! He knew all about thanking his back-up people. If his company increased its profits by even one percent, he gave a bonus to every single person in the company —secretaries and people in the mailroom, not just executives in offices. He appreciated each person for himself or herself, not just for the rank, not just as an engineer or a receptionist. It seemed to me that he was really thanking his back-up workers from his heart.

There are so many other people who help me sell cookies; the whole procedure is like a chain reaction. I couldn't do it without the help of the doormen in our apartment complex, for example. They're really my friends by now, and they stand up for me and do all they can to help. I'd love to be able to give them all cookies as presents, and I do when I can.

The people who bake our cookies have written me thank-you notes for selling so many of their cookies, but, again, the thank-you goes the other way, too. Their cookies are delicious, and their delivery is prompt. I'm the one who should be thanking them.

And the Girl Scouts, of course; they've helped me so much. I think everyone, or every girl anyway, would benefit from being a Girl Scout. You learn about all kinds of things in the Girl Scouts, then you get badges, which are like rewards for learning. I have badges for knowing about horses, camping, outdoor cooking, folk dance, drama (we did two plays), computers and math, and some others.

And mostly I have fun in the Girl Scouts— I've had the chance to do so many things I wouldn't otherwise have had the chance to do. My first troop leader, Barbara McLendon, was always encouraging me to try new things, and my troop leader now, Sandy Everson, is fabulous. She makes me feel like a big part of the troop.

When I think about the people who've backed me up in selling over the years, I'm amazed at how important some of them have become to my *whole* life, not just the selling part —Mr. Martin Edelston of *Boardroom Reports,* for instance, and Mr. Frank Baiamonte of the American Bankers Insurance Group. And Mr. Ben Feldman of the Million Dollar Round Table. And I also realize how the people who've helped me in other parts of my life, in lots of personal ways, have made it possible for me to do many things I've wanted to, including selling. Mrs. Mildred Berendson of the Chapin School and Mr. Robert Beshar are two people I especially think of that way.

You must have a lot of back-up people in your life, too, even your boss or the head of your company. Why not thank them today?

Now I've written this book—more back-up people to thank! If people hadn't written stories in newspapers about me all these years, the people at Random House, especially Becky Saletan, Annik LaFarge, Carolyn Reidy, and Melanie Fleishman, would never have heard about me or thought of the book! (Plus I wouldn't have had the chance to sell cookies at Random House.) Which reminds me—I'd like to thank Henry Wolf, Daniel Abraham, and Judy Loeser for making the book *look* like a winner (an important selling point!). And I would especially like to thank Cheryl Merser. We had a great time, talking about selling and going all over New York City watching selling in action; she helped me think about selling in some new ways—and to express what I've learned. And thank *you* for reading the book.

When you start thinking this way, it seems

that you can thank the entire world for one thing or another; that's a nice way to feel. And while you're at it, there's one more person to thank, and that's yourself! You're the one who's doing all the selling, so don't forget to be a little proud.

EPILOGUE

One of the best movies I ever saw was *Miracle on 34th Street*. It takes place at Christmastime, and the man who plays Santa Claus keeps telling everybody who comes to Macy's where the best places are to shop for whatever they want to buy; all this does is to draw more and more people to Macy's! And he would promise these gifts —like a respiratory machine for a retirement home—and somehow he would get them. He was a magical person.

In a way, salespeople can do the same thing, make people's dreams come true just by being kind and helping people get what they want. In real life, it costs money to make many dreams come true, so salespeople are a little different from Santa Claus, but they still can do a lot of good, help people get what they need, make them happy with what they buy and have a really good life themselves, too.

Is selling well a gift? If you love to sell, and you sell for a living, I would say it is a gift, because it's a gift to be able to enjoy what you do. But it's not a gift like being born a genius. Either you're a genius or not, nothing you can do about it, but with selling, you can keep on learning, keep getting better.

When I look back on my "career" so far in selling, I can see that I'm much more confident now than I was in the beginning. The more you sell, the more confident you get, then you sell even more and you keep getting more confident —it works like a math equation: experience + confidence = great selling.

Somebody recently asked me when I'd live if I had to live in any other time but now. I think I'd live in the future. So many interesting things are happening, and it would be fun to see how it all turns out. People will be selling things we've never even thought of, but they'll still be selling, just like they always have. . . . I wonder what I'll sell when I grow up . . . maybe . . . but wait, before you go, would you like to buy some Girl Scout cookies?

ABOUT THE AUTHORS

MARKITA ANDREWS was born in 1971. She joined the Girl Scouts at the age of six and has sold over 30,000 boxes of Girl Scout cookies to date. Her sales success has brought her appearances on major network news and talk shows and mention in newspapers and magazines across the nation, along with speaking engagements all over the United States and in Canada. In 1981 she starred in *The Cookie Kid*, a sales training film made by the Glyn Group for Walt Disney Productions. She attends Chapin School in New York City.

CHERYL MERSER worked in publishing for a number of years and is the author of *Honorable Intentions: The Manners of Courtship in the Eighties*. She lives in New York, where she is at work on a new book.